The Story of
Mother Jones

by Rachel A. Koestler-Grack

CHELSEA
CLUBHOUSE

An Imprint of Chelsea House Publishers

A Haights Cross Communications Company

Philadelphia

Chelsea Clubhouse books are published by Chelsea House Publishers, a subsidiary of Haights Cross Communications.

A Haights Cross Communications ✦ Company

Copyright © 2004 by Chelsea House Publishers. All rights reserved. No part of this publication may be reproduced or transmitted in any form or by any means without the written permission of the publisher.

The Chelsea House World Wide Web address is www.chelseahouse.com

Printed and bound in the United States of America.

9 8 7 6 5 4 3 2 1

Library of Congress Cataloging-in-Publication Data
Koestler-Grack, Rachel A., 1973–
  The story of Mother Jones / by Rachel A. Koestler-Grack.
     p. cm. — (Breakthrough biographies)
Summary: A biography of the labor leader who grew up in Ireland, emigrated to the United States, lost her family to yellow fever, and helped the mistreated working class, from coal miners to child mill workers, achieve better working conditions in the late 1800s and early 1900s.
Includes bibliographical references and index.
  ISBN 0-7910-7316-5
  1. Jones, Mother, 1843?–1930—Juvenile literature. 2. Women labor leaders—United States—Biography—Juvenile literature. 3. Women in the labor movement—United States—Biography—Juvenile literature.
4. Child labor—United States—History—Juvenile literature. 5. Labor movement—United States—Juvenile literature. [1. Jones, Mother, 1843?–1930. 2. Labor leaders. 3. Women—Biography.] I. Title. II. Series.
  HD8073.J6K64
2004331.88'092—dc21   2003000367

Selected Sources

Fetherling, Dale. *Mother Jones: The Miners' Angel*. Carbondale, Ill.: Southern Illinois University Press, 1974.

Gorn, Elliott J. *Mother Jones: The Most Dangerous Woman in America*. New York: Farrar, Straus, and Giroux, 2001.

Jones, Mary Harris. *The Autobiography of Mother Jones*. Chicago: Charles H. Kerr Publishing Company, 1990 [first published 1925].

Steel, Edward M., Editor. *The Speeches and Writings of Mother Jones*. Pittsburgh, Penn.: University of Pittsburgh Press, 1988.

Editorial Credits

Takeshi Takahashi, designer; Mary Englar, photo researcher; Jennifer Krassy Peiler, layout

Photo Credits

AP/Wide World: 29 (Jane Addams, Willa Cather and Juliette Low); ©Bettmann/CORBIS: title, 15, 16; ©CORBIS: cover, 4, 5, 12, 14, 20, 21, 23, 27; Denver Public Library:18, 25; Hulton Archive/Getty Image: 8,9,17; Illinois Labor Society: 26; Library of Congress: 29 (Harriet Tubman); North Wind Picture Archives: 6,7,10; ©Najlah Feanny/CORBIS SABA:19; Rick Apitz: back cover; Stock Montage, Inc.: 13, 22: ©Underwood & Underwood/CORBIS 24, 29 (Bessie Coleman)

Table of Contents

To America

Mary Harris was born in 1837 in Cork, Ireland. She was the second of five children. Like many Irish people at that time, Mary's family was very poor. They moved from their rural home to the city before Mary was born.

Mary's parents, Richard and Mary Harris, wanted a better life for themselves and for their children. When young Mary was about 10 years old, her father and older brother went to America. They found work doing hard **labor** and saved their **wages**. By the early 1850s, Mary's father was working for a railroad construction company and had earned enough money to bring his family to North America.

Many poor people in rural Ireland lived in cottages made of mud and straw. Before Mary was born, her family may have lived in a cottage like this one.

When Mary was a young woman, her family immigrated to Canada. Immigrants from Europe took crowded ships like the one pictured here, across the ocean to North America.

The family settled in Toronto, Canada, where a teenaged Mary attended public school. She was a bright girl and did well in school. At home, Mary helped her mother care for the household and learned to sew. To earn extra money for her family, Mary made clothes for neighbors and friends.

In 1857, when she was 20 years old, Mary enrolled in the Toronto Normal School. Here, she trained to be a teacher, one of the few jobs open to women at that time. Mary attended the school for one year, receiving enough training to find a job as a teacher in Toronto.

Dressmaking was one occupation that was open to women in the 1800s. Poor women could earn extra money by sewing dresses for wealthier women.

But Mary longed for adventure. In 1859, she left home to work as a teacher in Monroe, Michigan. In early 1860, she moved to Chicago, Illinois, and became a dressmaker. By the end of that year, she was off again, this time to a teaching job in Memphis, Tennessee.

In Memphis, Mary met and married George Jones. George was an iron molder. He worked in a factory that built and repaired products made out of iron. Mary and George rented a small house in a poor area of town. Most of their neighbors worked in factories and mills. They made low wages and struggled to survive.

George believed that workers deserved better treatment. He was a member and strong supporter of the International Iron Molders **Union**. The union brought together iron molders who wanted better wages and working conditions. As a group, they pressured their bosses to treat them fairly. Workers in other **trades** had also formed unions to fight for fair treatment.

Mary and George struggled, but they built a good life. Soon they had four children. Mary happily kept house and cared for her young children. At night, Mary listened to George talk about the Iron Molders Union. Together, Mary and George dreamed of a better life for themselves and for their children.

Steel mills were crowded and difficult environments to work in. Workers joined unions to pressure their bosses for better wages and working conditions.

Losing Everything

Yellow fever infected people in the South in the late 1860s. Wealthy and poor alike died from the disease. Here a wealthy girl plays alone in her house after her family has died of yellow fever.

In 1867, trouble came to Memphis. That year, a terrible disease known as yellow fever swept through the city. The citizens of Memphis panicked. Wealthy families fled for the countryside. But poor working people had no place to go.

The Jones's neighborhood was hit hard by yellow fever. Mary, George, and their children stayed in their home. They heard the cries of neighbors who came down with the disease. Each night, a horse-drawn cart traveled down their street. Families brought out their dead loved ones. Mary later remembered, "The dead surrounded us. They were buried at night quickly and without ceremony. All about my house I could hear weeping."

Then the terrible disease hit the Jones household. All four of Mary's children fell ill. She watched their skin turn yellow. She gently smoothed their hair as the fever rose and they vomited blood again and again. Within a few short days, all four children were dead. Then George became sick and died.

> *"I live in the United States, but I do not know exactly in what place…My address is like my shoes; it travels with me wherever I go."*
>
> —Mother Jones

In one week, Mary had lost her entire family. "I sat alone through nights of grief," she later wrote. "No one came to me. No one could. Other homes were as stricken as mine." As Mary sat in her dark and quiet home, she wondered why she had not become ill. Her whole family had caught yellow fever and died. But she still lived. Mary decided she had survived to help others.

During the winter of 1868, Mary Jones moved back to Chicago and started a dressmaking business. Most of Mary's customers came from wealthy families.

By the late 1800s, American cities were crowded with many factory workers. There was a great difference between the wealthy women who Mary made dresses for and the poor people she lived among.

The Great Chicago Fire spread through the city in 1871. It destroyed many buildings.

Mary later recalled, "Often while sewing for the lords and barons who lived in magnificent houses on the Lake Shore Drive, I would look out of the plate glass windows and see the poor, shivering wretches, jobless and hungry, walking along the frozen lake front." The differences between the rich and the poor troubled Mary. She wondered how some people could have so much while others worked so hard and had so little.

In 1871, a fire spread through Chicago. Known as the Great Chicago Fire, it destroyed Mary's dressmaking business. Now 34 years old, she would once again have to start over. Mary soon decided to become part of the labor struggle. She wanted to help working people improve their lives. Miners, factory workers, and mill employees often worked in dirty and dangerous conditions. Business owners paid their workers as little as possible.

Mary was known for her "motherly" appearance. She always wore a long black dress and her hair tied back in a neat bun.

Probably around the 1880s, Mary began attending nightly meetings of the Knights of Labor, then the largest union in the United States. She heard moving lectures about the need for fairer wages and better working conditions for America's labor force. She soon joined the union, eager to take up the fight.

Mary stood out in the Knights of Labor, where women were welcome but few were members. In her early 40s, Mary wore a long black dress, trimmed with lace and lavender velvet. She tied her white hair into a bun. Mary's simple, "motherly" appearance and her excellent speaking skills caught the attention of other union members. She quickly earned the respect of the men. They saw that behind Mary's motherly appearance, there was a powerful woman who was determined to improve the lives of workers.

The Great Railroad Strike

In 1873, the United States fell on hard economic times. The country was in a **depression**. Many workers lost their jobs, and their families ended up poor, hungry, and homeless. Railroad workers often held onto their jobs, but they saw their workdays grow longer and their wages shrink again and again.

In July 1877, the heads of four major railroad companies decided to cut their workers' pay by 10 percent. This was the breaking point for the workers. Railroad employees in West Virginia walked off the job first. Soon this **strike** spread along the railway lines from coast to coast, becoming the largest strike the nation had ever seen. In all, about 100,000 workers of all backgrounds—men and women, blacks, and whites—went on strike. In some cities, the strikes grew violent and turned into **riots**. The railroad strike lasted only two weeks, but it left 100 people dead and many more injured. In the end, the government stepped in and sided with the railroad companies.

The strike made a great impression on Mary Jones. The workers had sent a strong message to government and business leaders that they were tired of being mistreated. Mary began to believe that with more organization, strikers could change the role of labor in America.

These railroad workers in Martinsburg, West Virginia, were some of the first workers to walk off the job in the 1877 Baltimore and Ohio railroad strike. Sometimes these strikes turned into riots.

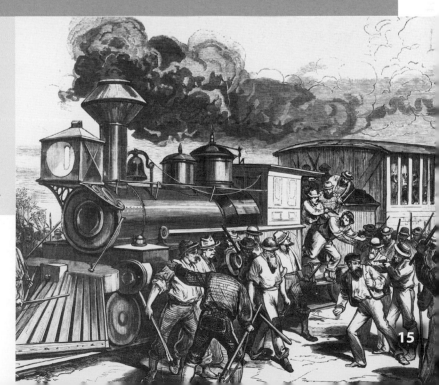

Victory for the Miners

The workers of Chicago and other cities organized strikes. During a strike, workers walked off their jobs and often marched in protest. They refused to return to work until the company improved their wage and working conditions. Some strikes became so violent that they had to be broken up by police. Mary decided that if workers were better organized, they could gain greater changes.

Mary began to travel across the country to attend workers' meetings. At the meetings, she spoke in a low, clear voice that inspired the workers. She was forceful and direct with her ideas. She later said, "The public is the sleepiest bunch you ever saw. You've got to wake them up! Then you get action." The workers respected Mary for her tireless work. They followed behind her like children. By the 1890s, people began calling her "Mother" Jones.

Mary traveled across the country and attended workers' meetings. Her rough talk inspired the workers to take action. She would say, "Pray for the dead, and fight like hell for the living."

The United Mine Workers (UMW) formed a union to look out for the needs of mine workers. Mine workers faced difficult conditions such as cave-ins, lung disease, and long hours.

She joined a new union called the United Mine Workers (UMW) in the 1890s. She traveled to mines in West Virginia, Alabama, and Pennsylvania. There she saw firsthand the dangers miners faced every day. Cave-ins could send rock crashing down on the miners. Freight cars that moved coal in and out of mines could crush workers who got in the way. Some miners developed lung diseases caused by breathing in thick coal dust. The miners often worked 14 hours a day, 6 days a week. Yet, they barely earned enough to survive. Many had to raise their families in rundown shacks.

Mother Jones asked them to join the UMW. She told them that many workers united would be a strong fighting force. The miners joined the union and staged strikes for better wages and working conditions.

> *"I'm not afraid of the pen, the sword or the scaffold. I will tell the truth...wherever I please."*
>
> —Mother Jones

Mother Jones had great talent for organizing strikes. When workers walked off the job, she found ways to keep mining families fed. She gave speeches and held rallies to boost the spirits of the workers. They called her the "Miners' Angel," and she called the workers "my boys." Mother Jones led children in parades and women in loud marches. The women banged on pots and pans and shouted in protest. They were grateful for the chance to stand up for their families.

Many coal companies gave in, bringing a shorter workday and higher wages for the miners. Mother Jones had shown her boys how working together they could make a difference.

Mother Jones had the ability to get whole families active in her causes. Here women march in support of UMW causes.

The Labor Movement

The labor movement in America started around the 1830s, during the **Industrial Revolution**. During this time, factory workers began using power-driven machinery to produce large quantities of goods. By the mid-1800s, workers were organizing into national unions. Over time, a few powerful unions emerged, including the Knights of Labor, the American Federation of Labor (AFL), the Industrial Workers of the World (IWW), and the Congress of Industrial Organizations (CIO).

The unions made some progress. But more often they suffered setbacks, as strikes failed and the government stood by business leaders. A turning point came during the Great Depression of the 1930s, when the United States suffered hard economic times. Americans thought if the workers had more money, they would buy more goods. This would be good for the economy. The government started favoring workers instead of businesses. Congress passed new laws in the 1930s that gave unions power and protection.

The labor movement in America has helped workers gain higher wages, shorter work hours, and better working conditions. Today, unions protect many types of workers, including teachers, nurses, and actors. America's largest and most powerful union organization is the AFL-CIO. This organization works for many local and national unions. About three-fourths of all union members in the country belong to the AFL-CIO.

Some of the powerful unions that emerged in the 1830s are still active today. The AFL-CIO still uses strikes to force employers to address workers' concerns.

The Children's March

Now famous as the Miners' Angel, Mother Jones took up the cause of another group of workers—children. By 1900, nearly 2 million children under the age of 16 had jobs in **textile** mills, factories, and mines. Mother Jones especially worried about the thousands of children who worked long hours in the textile mills. She believed children should be free to go to school and to play in the sun and fresh air.

In June 1903, Mother Jones went to Philadelphia, Pennsylvania, where mill workers were on strike. The strike had spread to 600 mills in the region. Among those who walked off the job were thousands of children. The strikers wanted their workweek reduced from 60 to 55 hours, even if it meant taking a cut in pay.

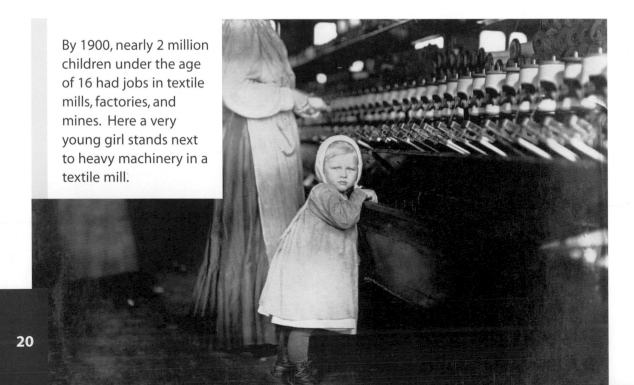

By 1900, nearly 2 million children under the age of 16 had jobs in textile mills, factories, and mines. Here a very young girl stands next to heavy machinery in a textile mill.

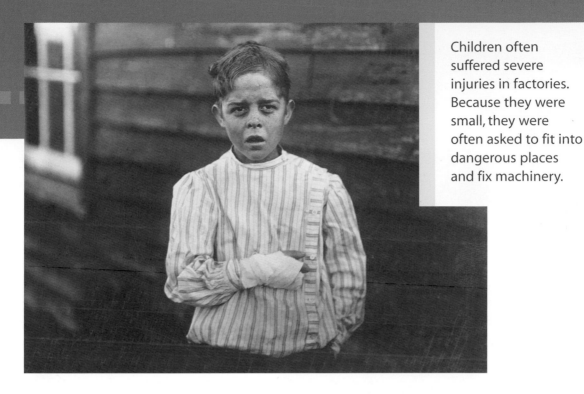

Children often suffered severe injuries in factories. Because they were small, they were often asked to fit into dangerous places and fix machinery.

Mother Jones planned to help the workers by stirring up public support for their cause. She led a large group of children and their parents through the streets of Philadelphia. Then she gave a speech. Mother Jones held up the arm of a boy. His hand was missing a finger. She then said, "Philadelphia's mansions were built on the broken bones, the quivering hearts, and drooping heads of these children." But the city's leaders refused to help the workers.

"I've done the best I could do to make the world a better place for poor, hard-working people."
—Mother Jones

Mary knew she needed the whole nation's attention to make a difference. She planned a march from Philadelphia all the way to New York City. "I am going to show Wall Street the flesh and blood from which it squeezes its wealth," she said. The trip would cover about 100 miles (160 kilometers) and end at President Theodore Roosevelt's summer home.

Theodore Roosevelt was president when Mother Jones organized her walking march. His secretary told Mother Jones he could do nothing to help her cause.

On July 7, 1903, Mother Jones began the walking march with 100 boys and girls, as well as many adult workers and labor leaders. The children's feet were sore from walking on dusty roads in the summer heat. Some marchers returned home.

The marchers sang songs and carried flags. Children held wooden signs that read "We Want Time to Play" and "We Only Ask for Justice." The group, which came to be known as "Mother Jones's Industrial Army," stopped in towns along the way. Thousands of people came to hear Mother Jones speak out.

The marchers reached New York City after nearly three weeks on the road. That night, thousands of New Yorkers watched Mother Jones and her followers march up Second Avenue. Three days later, Mother Jones spoke to a large crowd at Coney Island, an amusement park. "We want President Roosevelt to hear the wail of the children who never have a chance to go to school," she said.

On July 28, Mother Jones took three mill boys to President Roosevelt's home. But they were not allowed through the gates. The next day, Mother Jones wrote President Roosevelt a letter. She told him she would be happy to talk with him at any time he set. She wanted his help on behalf of the mill children. The president's secretary sent a reply saying that the president could do nothing to help.

After a few more days in New York, the marchers returned home. The strike ended, and the children went back to work. But Mother Jones and her marchers had helped working children get the attention of the nation. Some people called the event one of Mother Jones's greatest accomplishments. Over time, the awareness raised for child workers led to positive changes. In 1938, the U.S. Congress passed a labor law protecting children—35 years after the children's march.

Mother Jones played an important role in drawing attention to the issue of child labor. Public reaction was strongly against child labor. Eventually, the U.S. Congress had to pass laws protecting children.

A Dangerous Woman

Mother Jones continued to travel across the country to help mistreated workers. In 1905, she helped form the Industrial Workers of the World (IWW). This union brought together workers in different industries to fight for better working conditions. Of the union's leaders, Mother Jones was the only woman. Labor organizations were dangerous. Few other women were brave enough to take such an active role.

Mother Jones had become well known as a fierce fighter for working people. Many newspapers reported about her and the strikes she helped lead. She wrote articles and gave speeches all over the country in support of workers. But not everyone appreciated her work. Some people called her the most dangerous woman in America. They thought she was a troublemaker.

In 1914, when she was 77 years old, Mother Jones was arrested for helping miners strike in Colorado. She was locked in the cellar of a courthouse for nearly a month.

Mother Jones was one of the leaders for the IWW. This poster illustrated some of the concerns of the union.

The women pictured here marched in support of Mother Jones when she was imprisoned in 1914.

From jail, Mother Jones continued to write letters to workers and to newspapers. In a letter to a Denver, Colorado, newspaper, she wrote, "Of course I long to be out of jail. To be shut off from the sunlight is not pleasant." But jail did not make Mother Jones turn away from the workers. "I shall stand firm," she said.

Mother Jones slowed down in her later years. She suffered from rheumatism. This painful disease affects the joints and muscles. Although she did not get out among the workers as much, she remained famous. In 1925, she wrote the story of her life, called *The Autobiography of Mother Jones*. She enjoyed talking about her life and gave her last interview in the summer of 1930. Mother Jones was especially proud that many states were passing laws to protect child workers. "We've won out!" she said.

Mother Jones monument with "her boys on either side."

> *"The future is in labor's strong, rough hands."*
> —Mother Jones

Mother Jones died on November 30, 1930, when she was 93 years old. Thousands of people attended her funeral service at a miners' cemetery in Mount Olive, Illinois, where she was buried. The cemetery was dedicated to workers who had died in an 1898 strike. Mother Jones had said that she wanted to "sleep under the clay with those brave boys." She spent her life fighting for working people. Her fearless belief in the rights of workers inspired thousands of men, women, and children to stand up for themselves. Mother Jones proved that when they fought together, workers could change their lives.

Did You Know?

- Mother Jones always claimed she was born on May 1, 1830. But historians believe she was born in 1837.

- Mother Jones worked as a speaker for the Socialist Party. Socialists believed that communities should own land, factories, and other businesses. Then all people could share the money that the community property produced.

- In addition to working on behalf of coal miners and mill children, Mother Jones fought for copper miners in Arizona, telegraph operators in Chicago, garment workers in New York, and brewery workers in Milwaukee, Wisconsin.

- Mother Jones was known for her sharp wit. She once poked fun at President Theodore Roosevelt for having so many secret service men watching an "old woman and an army of children." She added, "You fellows do elect wonderful presidents. The best thing you can do is to put a woman in the next time."

- Mother Jones believed women gained power by speaking out. She once said, "You don't need a vote…You need convictions and a voice!" She wanted the poor to have the same rights and opportunities as the rich.

- In 1992, Mother Jones was entered into the U.S. Department of Labor Hall of Fame in Washington, D.C.

Mother Jones is pictured here with President Calvin Coolidge.

Important Dates

1837: Mary Harris is born in Cork, Ireland.

1857: Mary attends teachers college in Toronto, Canada.

1859: Mary moves to Monroe, Michigan.

1860: Mary moves to Chicago, Illinois, and then Memphis, Tennessee.

1861: Mary marries George Jones and learns about the Iron Molders Union. (age 24)

1862: Mary's and George's first child, Catherine, is born.

1863: Their second child, Elizabeth, is born.

1865: Son Terence is born.

1867: Youngest daughter, Mary, is born; yellow fever takes the lives of Mary's four children and husband, George. (age 30)

1868: Mary moves to Chicago and starts a dressmaking business. (age 31)

1871: The Great Chicago Fire destroys Mary's business; Mary becomes active in the fight for workers' rights.

1877: The first nation-wide strike of railroad workers begins.

1880s: Mary joins the Knights of Labor.

1890s: Mary becomes known as Mother Jones. She begins working for the United Mine Workers of America; she travels to mining towns to ask miners to join the union.

1894: Mother Jones visits clothing mills and observes working children. (age 57)

1903: Mother Jones leads the March of the Mill Children in July.

1905: Mother Jones helps form the Industrial Workers of the World.

1914: Mother Jones is put in jail in Colorado during a miners' strike.

1930: Mother Jones dies on November 30. (age 93)

Jane Addams (1860–1935)

Jane Addams was a social worker best known for founding Hull House in 1889, the first neighborhood social welfare agency in America. Located in Chicago, Hull House served the city's many immigrants. Addams also worked for such causes as child labor laws, women's rights, and public health. In 1931, she won the Nobel Prize for Peace.

Willa Cather (1873–1947)

Willa Cather is considered one of America's best fiction writers. Her finest books were *My Antonia* about an immigrant farm girl in Nebraska and *Death Comes for the Archbishop* about the work of a Catholic priest in the New Mexico Territory. In all, Cather wrote 12 books, which often expressed her deep love of the land and her belief in traditional family values.

Bessie Coleman (1892–1926)

Bessie Coleman was the first black woman in the world to be a licensed pilot, and the first black person to earn an international pilot's license. She traveled to France to learn to fly after flight instructors in the United States refused to teach a black woman. Coleman toured in air shows as a stunt pilot. She was killed when her plane crashed during a rehearsal.

Juliette Gordon Low (1860–1927)

Juliette Gordon Low founded the Girl Scouts of America in 1912 in Savannah, Georgia. She set up a national headquarters for the organization in Washington, D.C., and traveled throughout the country to raise money and organize troops. By the time of her death in 1927, there were 140,000 girl scouts and troops in every state.

Harriet Tubman (1822–1913)

Born a slave in Maryland, Harriet Tubman escaped to the North in 1849. Unlike other escaped slaves, she dared to return to the South to guide other slaves north to freedom on the Underground Railroad. During the Civil War (1861–1865), Tubman served the Union Army as a nurse and a scout. She spent her later years helping former slaves.

Glossary

cotton mill (KOT-uhn mil) a building where workers use machinary to turn cotton into fabric

depression (dih-PRESH-uhn) a period when businesses do poorly and many people lose their jobs

Industrial Revolution (in-DUSS-tree-uhl rev-uh-LOO-shun) the time when the introduction of power-driven machinery changed the way that people made goods; the Industrial Revolution started in Europe in the late 1700s and spread to the United States by the early 1800s.

labor (LAY-bur) hard work; also, the people employed to do work.

riot (RYE-uht) a gathering of people that is noisy, violent, and hard to control

strike (STRIKE) when a group of workers refuses to go to their jobs to protest low pay or poor working conditions

textile (TEK-stile) cloth that has been woven or knitted; workers in textile mills operate machines that weave materials such as cotton or silk into cloth.

trade (TRAYD) a certain job or craft that is done by hand or by machine

union (YOON-yuhn) an organized group of workers formed to improve working conditions, pay, health benefits, or any other circumstances involved in a job

wage (WAYJ) the money someone is paid to do work

To Learn More

READ THESE BOOKS

Nonfiction

Colman, Penny. *Mother Jones and the March of the Mill Children.* Brookfield, Conn.: Millbrook Press, 1994.

Currie, Stephen. *We Have Marched Together: The Working Children's Crusade.* Minneapolis: Lerner Publications Company, 1997.

Hawxhurst, Joan C. *Mother Jones: Labor Crusader.* Austin, Tex.: Raintree Steck-Vaughn, 1994.

Kraft, Betsy Harvey. *Mother Jones: One Woman's Fight for Labor.* New York: Clarion Books, 1995.

Fiction

Bartoletti, Susan Campbell. *Kids on Strike!* Boston: Houghton Mifflin Co., 1999.

Cohn, Diana. *¡Sí, Se Puede! Yes, We Can!* El Paso, Tex.: Cinco Puntos Press, 2002.

McCully, Emily Arnold. *The Bobbin Girl.* New York: Dial Books for Young Readers, 1996.

LOOK UP THESE INTERNET SITES

Coal Mining in the Gilded Age and Progressive Era

www.cohums.ohio-state.edu/history/projects/LaborConflict/OnStrike/
Look at historical photographs and illustrations or read the articles about the lives of coal miners in the late 1800s and early 1900s. Discover the reasons why miners went on strike.

Free the Children

www.freethechildren.org
Learn about this international organization for kids who want to speak out against child labor and for children's rights around the world.

The History Place: Child Labor in America

www.historyplace.com/unitedstates/childlabor
View historical photographs of children forced to work in situations ranging from coal mines to factories to farms. Learn more about what their lives were like.

Mother Jones

www.aflcio.org/aboutaflcio/history/history/jones.cfm
Read a short biography about Mother Jones and follow the links to learn more about the movement toward organizing labor unions.

Mother Jones Biography

www.newsday.com/news/education/sbp/ny-sbp_62503x,0,634671.story?coll=ny-sbp-headlines
Review another biography about Mother Jones and check out links to photographs and more information about her life.

Internet search key words:

Mother Jones, American labor movement, labor unions, Great Railroad Strike

Index